# Sock
## Puppets

This edition published in 2013
By SpiceBox™
12171 Horseshoe Way
Richmond, BC
Canada V7A 4V4

First published in 2012
Copyright © SpiceBox™ 2012
Text and photographs copyright © Didier Carpentier 2011

ISBN 10: 1-77132-024-9
ISBN 13: 978-1-77132-024-5

CEO and Publisher: Ben Lotfi
Author: Cendrine Armani
Editorial: Cynthia Nugent
Creative Director: Garett Chan
Art Director: Christine Covert
Design & Layout: Charmaine Muzyka & Kirsten Reddecopp
Production: Mell D'Clute & James Badger
Sourcing: Janny Lam

For more SpiceBox products and information, visit our website:
www.spiceboxbooks.com

Manufactured in China

3 5 7 9 10 8 6 4 2

# Contents

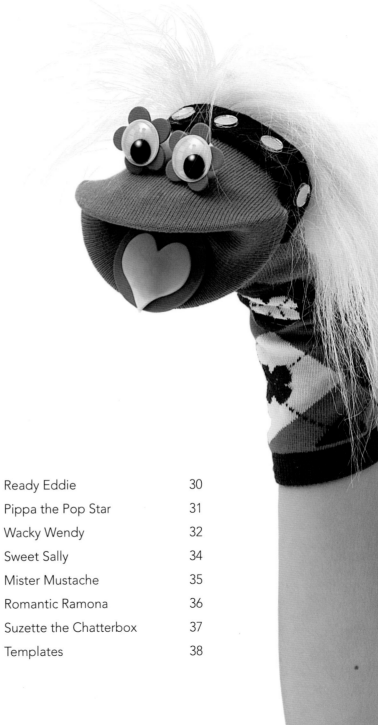

# Materials & Embellishments

Making sock puppets is a fabulously creative activity, because you can use any type of craft supplies you have around your home.

Here is a list of items that are used in this book, but remember you can use anything that inspires you!

- single socks - plain or patterned, ankle or long
- pipe cleaners
- pom-poms
- faux fur
- scissors
- googly eyes
- strong craft glue
- craft embellishments such as gemstones, sticky-backed mirrors, buttons, and sequins
- angel hair – white
- plastic laces
- mini feather boa – black
- felt pieces
- craft foam sheets
- glue dots
- cardboard – 1 mm thick

# The Technique in Pictures

All the projects in this book are based on the steps to make Lola the Mouse.  Refer back to this project whenever you need to remember how to make the mouth of your puppet.   You can, of course, experiment with other shapes and sizes of cardboard inserts to create different puppets.   Start with a sock of your choice, make the mouth insert out of cardboard, and then add whatever decorative details you like to bring your character to life.   Use your imagination!

# Lola
## the Mouse

### Materials:

- 1 grey sock
- cardboard
- scissors
- felt – white
- craft foam sheets – pink, magenta and grey
- pom-poms – 2 white, 1 pink
- plastic lace – grey
- googly eyes

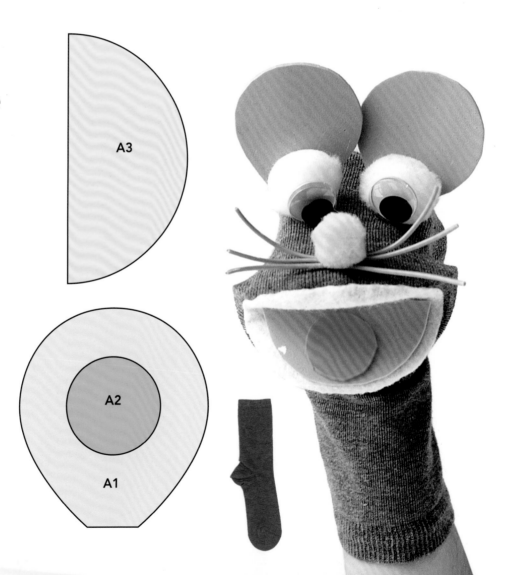

A3

A2

A1

**1**

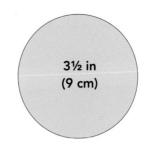

3½ in
(9 cm)

**1.** Start by cutting a 3½ in (9 cm) diameter cardboard circle.

**2**

**2.** Fold it in half, crease the fold well.

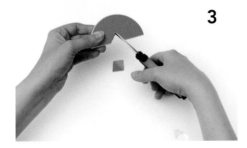

**3**

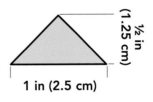

½ in (1.25 cm)

1 in (2.5 cm)

**3.** Find the center of the fold line and cut out a triangle approximately 1 in (2.5 cm) wide and ½ in (1.25 cm) tall.

**4**

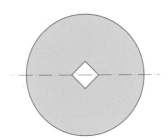

**4.** You now have a pair of jaws with a square hole in the middle.

**5.** Hold the folded jaws in one hand and ease them into the foot of the sock.

**6.** Pull the sock up your arm. Slide the cardboard to the toe of the sock, rotating the sock on your arm so the heel is facing up. Your knuckles will fit there. Open the jaws.

**7.** Push the toe of the sock into the jaws, poking some sock through the square hole in the jaws.

**8.** With the fingers of your inside hand, gently pull the toe through to the inside of the sock. Hold the jaws in place while you pull.

**9.** Continue to pull the toe through the jaws until you get the desired shape for the head. The knuckles should fit inside the heel of the sock, and you should be be able to open and close the jaws like a mouth.

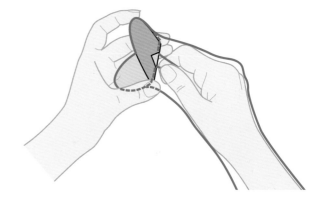

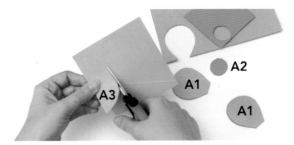

**10.** Take your hand out of the sock leaving the jaws inside. Cut a white felt circle 3 in (7.5 cm) in diameter. Position it on the inside mouth, then glue the felt in place.

**11.** Using the templates on page 6, cut shapes from the foam sheets: grey for the ears (A1), pink for the inside of the mouth (A3), and dark pink for the tongue (A2).

**12.** Cut three 4 in (10 cm) lengths of plastic lace. Gather these together and glue them together in the middle along with the pink pom-pom to create the nose and whiskers. Glue eyes onto the white pom-poms.

**13.** Put your hand inside the sock again. Position the eyes, nose and whiskers until you are happy with the arrangement. Memorize where everything went or mark the positions with safety pins.

**14.** Using strong craft glue or glue dots, glue the back of each feature, then hold them in place one by one, maintaining light pressure for a minute to allow the glue to set.

# Chloe
## the Giraffe

**Materials:**

- 1 long sock - brown and beige
- cardboard
- scissors
- felt – brown
- craft foam sheets – red, brown, black
- pom-poms – 4 medium brown, 2 small beige
- pipe cleaner – 5½ in (14 cm)
- faux fur – brown
- googly eyes
- strong craft glue or glue dots

**Instructions:**

Begin by cutting out a 3½ in (9 cm) diameter circle of cardboard, then follow steps 2–9 on pages 7 and 8.

Cut a 3 in (7.5 cm) diameter circle from the brown felt and glue it to the inside of the mouth.

For the tongue, cut out red craft foam in the shape of template J1 on page 39. Cut out two black craft-foam eyelashes using the J2 shapes on the same page. Cut 2 ears out of brown foam using pattern J3.

Glue the eyes onto the eyelashes, then stick these onto brown pom-poms. To make the horns, glue the remaining two brown pom-poms onto the pipe cleaner, one on either end. For the horns, bend the pipe cleaner into a "U" and glue by the middle onto the head. Follow steps 13 and 14 on page 9 to attach the features to the sock. Glue the faux fur between the horns.

Fold together the bottoms of the ears and glue them on.

# Bob
## the Fish

### Materials:

- 1 patterned sock – blue and mauve
- cardboard
- scissors
- craft foam sheets – violet, blue
- pom-poms – 2 purple
- googly eyes
- strong craft glue or glue dots

### Instructions:

Begin by cutting out a 3½ in (9 cm) diameter circle of cardboard, then follow steps 2–9 on pages 7 and 8.

Cut out the tongue using template B1 (page 38) in purple craft foam, then in blue foam cut out a dorsal fin using the G1 shape. Still using the blue foam, cut out 2 gills in the G2 shapes. Cut fringes into the gills. Glue the googly eyes onto the pom-poms, then follow steps 13 and 14 on page 9 to complete Bob the Fish.

# Justine
## the Frog

### Materials:

- 1 patterned sock – green and white
- cardboard
- scissors
- felt – red
- craft foam sheets - white and green
- pom-poms – 2 yellow
- faux fur – yellow
- googly eyes
- strong craft glue or glue dots

### Instructions:

Begin by cutting out a 3½ in (9 cm) diameter circle of cardboard, then follow steps 2–9 on pages 7 and 8.

Use red felt to make a 2¾ in (7 cm) circle for the inside of the mouth and glue it on. Cut out 2 eye sockets from a sheet of green craft foam using the B1 template (page 38). Cut out the tongue in white foam using the B2 template. Glue the eyes on the green circles and glue those onto the yellow pom-poms. Follow steps 13 and 14 on page 9 to attach the features and hair.

# Sandra
## the Zebra

## Materials:

- 1 black-and-white striped sock
- cardboard
- scissors
- craft foam sheets – orange, fuschia, mauve and black
- pom-poms – 2 pale blue
- faux fur – black
- googly eyes
- gemstones – 2 pink
- strong craft glue or glue dots

## Instructions:

Begin by cutting out a 3½ in (9 cm) diameter circle of cardboard, then follow steps 2–9 on pages 7 and 8.

Cut a circle 2¾ in (7 cm) in diameter out of the orange foam sheet. Cut a B1 shape (page 38) in fuschia foam for the tongue. Finally, cut a pair of glasses in purple foam using the C1 template.

Using a black foam sheet, cut out 2 lenses using the C2 template, and two C3 eyelash shapes.

Glue the googly eyes onto the eyelashes, then glue these onto the blue pom-poms. Glue the pom-poms to the the bottom of the glasses and apply the gemstones to the corners of the glasses. Follow steps 13 and 14 on page 9 to attach the features and hair.

# Paul
## the Lion

## Materials:

- 1 patterned sock – orange and brown paw print
- cardboard
- scissors
- felt pieces – 1 white, 1 brown
- craft foam sheets –orange, red
- faux fur – brown
- googly eyes
- strong craft glue or glue dots

## Instructions:

Begin by cutting out a 3½ in (9 cm) diameter circle of cardboard, then follow steps 2–9 on pages 7 and 8.

Cut a large circle out of white felt. In brown foam cut out a 1½ in (4 cm) diameter circle. Glue the white circle to the inside of the mouth. Glue the brown circle in the center of the white circle.

Cut the tongue using form F3 and red craft form (templates on page 38). For the ears, cut two E1 shapes in orange foam. Glue on the eyes and ears, and the fur on the head.

# Maggie
## the Cow

## Materials:

- 1 patterned black and white sock
- cardboard
- scissors
- felt – black, red
- craft foam sheets – pink, fuschia and white
- pom-poms – 2 black, 1 yellow
- faux fur – black
- cow pattern fabric cut into a triangle scarf shape
- googly eyes
- strong craft glue or glue dots

## Instructions:

Begin by cutting out a 3½ in (9 cm) diameter circle of cardboard, then follow steps 2–9 on pages 7 and 8.

Cut a 3 in (7 cm) diameter circle from the red felt, and a 1½ in (4 cm) diameter circle from the black felt. of black felt. Glue them into the mouth of the puppet.

For the nose, cut out the D1 shape (page 38) in pink foam. Use the D2 template to cut out a flower shape in fuschia craft foam, and finally, cut out a white foam circle using the B2 template for the uvula (that little punching bag in the throat).

Next, from the black felt, cut out two D3 forms for the ears, and two D4 shapes for the horns. Glue the black pom-poms on the nose and the yellow pom-pom in the center of the flower. Follow steps 13 and 14 on page 9 to glue everything on. To complete Maggie, wrap the scarf around her head and tie it under her chin.

# Groovin' Gary

## Materials:

- 1 striped sock – blue and green
- 1 white sock
- cardboard
- scissors
- craft foam sheets – black, red, green, white
- pom-poms – blue
- felt – black, red
- faux fur – black
- googly eyes
- strong craft glue or glue dots

## Instructions:

Begin by cutting out a 3½ in (9 cm) diameter circle of cardboard and follow steps on pages 7 and 8.

With the black craft foam, cut out a 2¾ in (7 cm) diameter circle for the inside of the mouth. Cut out a tongue shape in red foam using the E1 template on page 37. Finally, cut out the nose from green craft foam using the B2 shape.

Cut out two fangs in white foam using the E2 shape. Follow steps 13 and 14 on page 9 for gluing everything on. Glue the fur on the head, roll up the white sock to form a cap, glue it over the hair, and finish it off by gluing the blue pom-pom on top.

# Sam
## the Snake

## Materials:

- 1 patterned sock – yellow, pink and black
- cardboard
- scissors
- felt – orange
- craft foam sheets – fuchsia, green, purple, yellow, orange, blue, red
- pom-poms – 2 pink
- 2 googly eyes
- strong craft glue or glue dots

## Instructions:

Begin by cutting out a 3½ in (9 cm) diameter circle of cardboard, then follow steps 2–9 on pages 7 and 8.

For the inside of the mouth, cut a 3¼ in (8.25 cm) diameter circle in the orange felt. Fold it in half and make a 1/2 in (1.25 cm) slit in the center and along the fold. Glue into the mouth. Cut an F1 shape (page 38) from the fuchsia foam and glue it inside the mouth.

Next, using the purple craft foam and the F2 template, cut out the tongue. Insert the end of the tongue through the slit. Cut two each of the templates F1, B1, E1 and F3 in the different craft foam colors for the eyes (see photo). Arrange two piles of foam circles by decreasing size, glue them together, then glue them onto the two pom-poms. Glue on googly eyes. Follow steps 13 and 14 on page 9 to complete Sam the Snake.

# Kooky
# Kevin

## Materials:

- 1 patterned sock – mauve and black
- cardboard
- scissors
- felt – white, pink
- craft foam sheets – red, purple, black
- pom-poms – 2 black, 1 purple
- faux fur – black
- googly eyes
- strong craft glue or glue dots

## Instructions:

Begin by cutting out a 3½ in (9 cm) diameter circle of cardboard, then follow steps 2–9 on pages 7 and 8.

Cut out a 3 in (7.5 cm) diameter circle in white felt for the mouth.

Cut out a 2 in (5 cm) diameter circle in pink felt and glue it into the mouth.

To make the tongue, cut out red craft foam using the F3 template on page 38, then in purple foam cut out two B1 shapes for the eye sockets. Then cut out 2 black craft foam eyelashes using pattern H.

Glue the purple eye sockets onto the eyelashes, and the googly eyes onto the purple eye sockets, then glue these onto the pom-poms. Follow steps 13 and 14 on page 9. Glue the faux fur onto the head.

# Strawberry
# Stacey

## Materials:

- 1 patterned sock – white with red polka dots
- cardboard
- scissors
- felt – green, red, yellow
- craft foam sheet – yellow
- googly eyes
- strong craft glue or glue dots

## Instructions:

Begin by cutting out a 3½ in (9 cm) diameter circle of cardboard, then follow steps 2–9 on pages 7 and 8.

Cut a 3 in (7.5 cm) diameter circle out of green felt. From red felt cut a circle 1¼ in (3.2 cm) in diameter. First apply the green, then the red felt to the inside of the mouth.

Cut out yellow craft foam for the tongue using the template K1 on page 39. Cut the leaf hat out of green felt using the K2 form. Then for the stem use K2. Cut a slit in the leaf where indicated on the template, push the end of the stem through it.

Cut 1¾ in (3 mm) leaf veins out of yellow felt.  Glue them to the leaf.

Follow steps 13 and 14 on page 9 to attach the features and complete the puppet.

# Lovely
# Lucy

## Materials:

- 1 patterned sock – black with purple and fuchsia
- cardboard
- scissors
- felt – black
- craft foam sheets – fuschsia, mauve, bright green and white
- googly eyes
- faux fur – black
- strong craft glue or glue dots

## Instructions:

Begin by cutting out a 3½ in (9 cm) diameter circle of cardboard, then follow steps 2–9 on pages 7 and 8.

Cut out a B1 (page 38) shape for the inside of the mouth from a fuchsia foam sheet, then a tongue out of mauve craft foam using template E1.

Cut two D1 shapes for the eye sockets, one from a mauve and the second from a fuchsia foam sheet. Cut out 2 white foam F3 shapes for the whites of the eyes.

Cut out the glasses from a sheet of bright green craft foam (C1). Refer to Steps 13 and 14 on page 9 to glue the eyes, glasses and hair on.

# Flavia
## the Cool Kid

### Materials:

- 1 striped sock – black and purple
- cardboard
- scissors
- craft foam sheets – mauve, pink, white, black
- pom-poms – 2 pink
- 2 musical notes – sparkly black
- pipe cleaner – pink
- plastic lace – pink
- faux fur – black
- googly eyes
- strong craft glue or glue dots

### Instructions:

Begin by cutting out a 3½ in (9 cm) diameter circle of cardboard.
Take the striped sock and follow steps 2–9 on pages 7 and 8.

Cut out an L1 shape (page 39) from a sheet of mauve craft foam for the inside of the mouth, and from the pink foam, cut out a tongue shape using the L2 form.

Cut teeth out of the white craft foam using form L3, and from the black craft foam cut a nose using the B2 (page 38) pattern. Cut out a pink foam 1½ x 1 in (4 x 2.5 cm) rectangle and glue the music notes on it. Cut 2 pieces of plastic lace and glue the ends to the back of the pink rectangle. Glue a pink pom-pom to each end of the pipe cleaner to make headphones. Glue the other ends of the lace to the back of the headphone pom-poms.

Follow steps 13 and 14 on page 9 to glue on the hair and headphones.

23

# Shy
# Marie

## Materials:

- 1 plaid sock – grey and white
- 1 grey sock
- cardboard
- scissors
- craft foam sheets – pink, white
- felt – grey
- pom-poms – 2 pink
- googly eyes
- strong craft glue or glue dots

## Instructions:

Begin by cutting out a 3½ in (9 cm) diameter circle of cardboard, then follow steps 2–9 on pages 7 and 8.

Cut out a 2¾ in (7 cm) diameter circle from piece of grey felt and apply it to the inside of the mouth. For the tongue, use template E1 on page 38 to cut out a shape from the sheet of pink craft foam, and template F3 for a circle in white foam. Glue these together, then glue both onto the grey mouth. Take the grey sock and cut off the foot. Slide the upper part of the sock over the puppet's head and fold under the raw edge around the face to make a hood.

Follow steps 13 and 14 on page 9 to finish Marie.

# Nautical Nick

## Materials:

- 1 striped sock – blue and white
- 1 white sock
- cardboard
- scissors
- felt – blue
- craft foam sheets – red, white
- pom-pom – red
- faux fur – black
- twist tie
- googly eyes
- strong craft glue or glue dots

## Instructions:

Begin by cutting out a 3½ in (9 cm) diameter circle of cardboard, then follow steps 2–9 on pages 7 and 8.

Cut out a circle following pattern B1 (page 38) in red craft foam, and form K1 (page 39) in white craft foam for the tongue. Glue into the mouth.

To make the beret, cut a cardboard circle diam. 2³/4 in (7 cm). Insert cardboard in the white sock. Tighten the sock flush against the cardboard and secure it with a twist tie. Cut off extra sock. Cut a ¹/4 x 6 in (0.6 x 16 cm) strip of blue felt. Glue it on to the top and bottom of the beret. Glue on the red pom-pom.

Refer to Steps 13 and 14 on page 9 to complete gluing the parts onto Malo.

# Surfer
# Dave

## Materials:
- 1 patterned sock – grey with black polka dots
- cardboard
- scissors
- craft foam sheets – black, red, blue
- pom-poms – 2 white
- faux fur – grey
- strong craft glue or glue dots

## Instructions:

Begin by cutting out a 3½ in (9 cm) diameter circle of cardboard, then follow steps 2–9 on pages 7 and 8.

Cut a 3½ in (9 cm) diameter circle out of the black craft foam sheet for the interior of the mouth, then a tongue out of red craft foam using template B1 on page 38.

Cut out the sunglasses from a sheet of blue craft foam (C1), and for the dark lenses cut two C2 shapes out of black foam. Glue one side of the lenses to the back of the glasses and the other onto the white pom-poms.

Refer to Steps 13 and 14 on page 9 to complete the sock puppet. Glue the faux fur behind the white pom-poms.

# Jojo
## the Cobra

### Materials:

- 1 striped sock – khaki, green and fuchsia
- cardboard
- scissors
- felt – white, brown
- craft foam sheets – brown, fuchsia
- pom-pom – green
- faux fur – brown
- googly eyes
- strong craft glue or glue dots

### Instructions:

Begin by cutting out a 3½ in (9 cm) diameter circle of cardboard, then follow steps 2–9 on pages 7 and 8.

For the mouth, use the B1 template (page 38) to cut a shape from the brown craft foam. Cut the tongue from the fuchsia foam using the M template. Poke the end of the tongue into the hole at the back of the mouth (this is the center square you cut out of the cardboard jaw on p.7). Refer to Steps 13 and 14 on page 9 to complete gluing on the features and the hair.

# Cutie Pie
## Eva

### Materials:

- 1 patterned sockette – animal fur pattern in grey, white, and black
- 1 black sock
- cardboard
- scissors
- felt – green, red, yellow, mauve, fuchsia
- craft foam sheets – hot pink, red, black
- feather boa – mini black
- googly eyes
- strong craft glue or glue dots

### Instructions:

Begin by cutting out a 3½ in (9 cm) diameter circle of cardboard. Pull the patterned sockette over the foot of the black sock, then follow steps 2–9 on pages 7 and 8.

For the flower, cut green felt in the N1 shape (page 38), and cut the N2 shape in purple felt. Use F3 pattern and fuchsia for the center of the flower. Glue the flower pieces together.

Make eye sockets, by cutting two E1 shapes out of a sheet of black craft foam. Glue on the eyes. Cut an N3 shape for the inside of the mouth from the hot pink foam. Cut the tongue from red craft foam using the K1 pattern.

Referring to Steps 13 and 14 on page 9, glue on the eyes, the inside of the mouth, the tongue, and the boa on top of the head.

# Ready
# Eddie

## Materials:

- 1 black sock
- cardboard
- scissors
- craft foam sheets – yellow, green, blue, red
- pom-pom – purple
- faux fur – orange
- googly eyes
- strong craft glue or glue dots

## Instructions:

Begin by cutting out a 3½ in (9 cm) diameter circle of cardboard, then follow steps 2–9 on pages 7 and 8.

Cut out yellow craft foam using the L1 (page 39) template for the mouth, then in the red foam follow the P template for the tongue. Glue in the mouth and the tongue.

For the eye sockets, use the B1 template (page 38) and cut one each out of the blue and green craft foams. Glue the eyes on the sockets.

Follow steps 13 and 14 on page 9 to complete adding Ready Eddie's features and hair.

# Pippa
## the Pop Star

## Materials:

- 1 patterned sock: dark purple, purple and white argyle
- cardboard
- scissors
- felt – dark purple
- craft foam sheets – white, purple
- pom-poms  – 2 white
- faux fur – white
- mirrors or gemstones - 5 self-adhesive
- googly eyes
- strong craft glue or glue dots

## Instructions:

Begin by cutting out a 3½ in (9 cm) diameter circle of cardboard, then follow steps 2–9 on pages 7 and 8. Take off the sock.

Cut two D2 shapes (page 38) for the eye sockets from the purple craft foam.  Also use purple craft foam for the tongue following the F1 shape. Then cut a white foam O2 (page 39) heart shape. Glue it onto the purple tongue and glue these inside the mouth.

Glue the eyes on the sockets and glue these two onto the white pom-poms. Cut the dark purple headband strip and stick on the mirrors. Refer to Steps 13 and 14 on page 9 to finish gluing the features, hair and headband onto Leon.

# Wacky
# Wendy

## Materials:
- 1 patterned sock – grey with pink spots
- cardboard
- scissors
- craft foam sheets – fuchsia, white, purple
- pom-poms – 2 sparkly, grey
- faux fur – grey
- googly eyes
- lace trim – white
- strong craft glue or glue dots

## Instructions:

Begin by cutting out a 3½ in (9 cm) diameter circle of cardboard, then follow steps 2–9 on pages 7 and 8.

Cut the tongue from a sheet of fuchsia craft foam, using the O1 pattern (page 38), then cut out the teeth from a sheet of white craft foam using the O2 template. Cut a strip for the headband from the purple craft foam.

Glue the lace onto the edge of hairband. Glue the eyes on the pom-poms and refer to steps 13 and 14 on page 9 to complete gluing the features, headband, and faux fur.

# Sweet Sally

## Materials:

- 1 striped sock – hot pink and white
- cardboard
- scissors
- craft foam sheets – hot pink and white
- pom-poms – 2 white
- felt – white, pink
- faux fur – white
- googly eyes
- strong craft glue or glue dots

## Instructions:

Begin by cutting out a 3½ in (9 cm) diameter circle of cardboard, then follow steps 2–9 on pages 7 and 8.

Cut out a 3 in (7 cm) diameter circle in white felt for the mouth.

Cut out a tongue shape using template B1 on page 38 in hot pink craft foam and glue it in the center of the white mouth circle. Then in white foam, cut out form B2 for the uvula (that little punching bag in the throat).

Glue the eyes onto the pom-poms.

Make Rhianna's bow – Cut a 10½ x 1 in (27 x 2.5 cm) band in pink felt and another one in white felt. Line up the bands and press them together.

Cut two more strips out of the pink felt and the white felt.
This time, make them 2½ x ⅓ in (0.8 x 6 cm). Take off the backing and press the strips together. To create the appearance of a tied bow, take the ends of the long strip and fold them into the center and out again (see diagram). Glue the folds in place and wrap the short strip around the middle, white side out. Follow steps 13 and 14 on page 9. Glue the faux fur onto the head.

# Mister Mustache

## Materials:

- 1 knitted stocking – orange and brown stripes
- cardboard
- scissors
- craft foam sheets – red, orange
- pom-poms – 2 brown, 1 orange
- faux fur – brown
- googly eyes
- strong craft glue or glue dots

## Instructions:

Begin by cutting out a 3½ in (9 cm) diameter circle of cardboard, then follow steps 2–9 on pages 7 and 8.

Use form B1 (page 38) for a tongue cut from a red foam sheet and glue it inside the mouth.

Cut three B1 shapes out of a sheet of orange foam for the eye sockets and the tongue. Then cut a red craft foam uvula (that little punching bag at the back of your throat) using template F3 on page 5. Glue it onto the orange foam tongue.

Glue the eyes onto the pom-poms, glue these onto the eye sockets.

Cut two pieces of faux fur for the two halves of the mustache and glue on as in the photo. Stick on the orange pom-pom for the nose. Cut a piece of faux fur for the head and glue on.

Refer to Steps 13 and 14 on page 9 to complete.

# Romantic
# Ramona

## Materials:

- 1 striped sock – red, fuchsia, pink and white
- cardboard
- scissors
- felt – black
- craft foam sheets – fuchsia, white, pink, red
- pom-poms – 2 white
- faux fur – black
- googly eyes
- strong craft glue or glue dots

## Instructions:

Begin by cutting out a 3½ in (9 cm) diameter circle of cardboard, then follow steps 2–9 on pages 7 and 8.

Cut out a circle of black felt 2¾ in (7 cm) in diameter. Glue it to the inside of the mouth. Cut out pink and fuchsia craft foams for the heart shape (O2 on page 38). Then in each of white and red foam cut F1 shapes for the eye sockets. Finally, in white and red craft foams, cut an E1 and a B2 template for the tongue.

In the color combinations shown in the photograph, glue the eyes onto the hearts, the hearts onto the sockets, and the sockets to the pom-poms. Glue these to the head. Glue in the tongue and the faux fur to the top of the head.

# Suzette
## the Chatterbox

### Materials:

- 1 patterned sock – blue with white polka dots
- cardboard
- scissors
- felt – white
- craft foam sheets – red, black
- pom-poms – 2 blue
- angel hair – white
- 2 googly eyes
- strong craft glue or glue dots

### Instructions:

Begin by cutting out a 3½ in (9 cm) diameter circle of cardboard, then follow steps 2–9 on pages 7 and 8.

Cut a 2¾ in (7 cm) diameter circle out of white foam. Glue to the inside of the mouth. Cut out the tongue from the red foam sheet using form B1 (page 38). Glue into the mouth.

In black foam cut out a pair of glasses using the C1 template.

Cut the eye sockets out of white felt using the E1 pattern. Glue the eyes onto the pom-poms, then glue these onto the eye sockets.

Refer to Steps 13 and 14 on page 9 to help you complete Suzette the Chatterbox. Glue on the angel hair.

# Templates

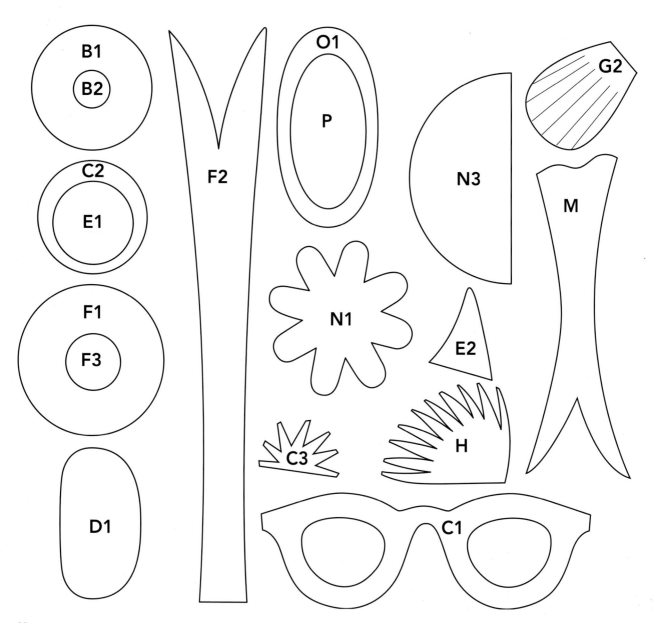

B1

B2

C2

E1

F1

F3

D1

F2

O1

P

N1

C3

H

E2

N3

G2

M

C1

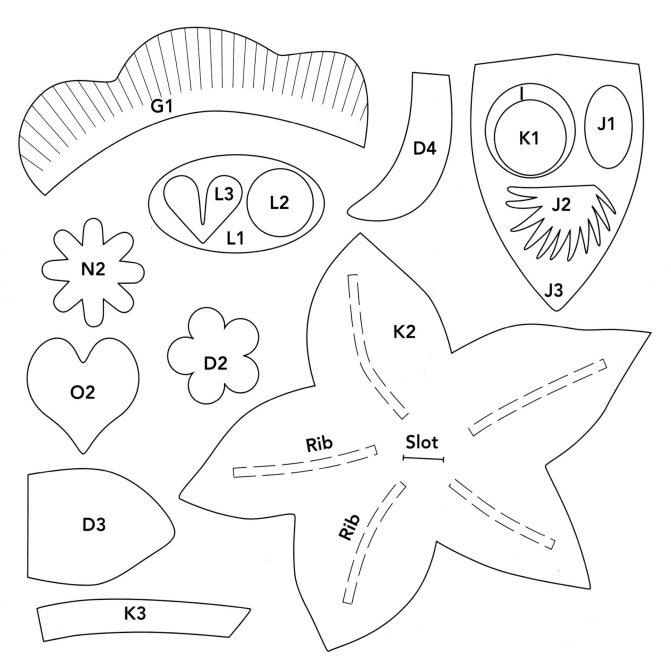

G1

D4

K1

J1

J2

J3

L3

L2

L1

N2

K2

D2

O2

Rib

Slot

Rib

D3

K3